D1480254

Basic Domestic Reptile & Amphibian Library

Chameleons

W. Schmidt, K. Tamm and W. Wallikewitz

Published in association with T.F.H. Publications, Inc.,
the world's largest and most respected publisher of pet literature

Chelsea House Publishers
Philadelphia

CONTENTS

Basic Domestic Reptile and Amphibian Library

Box Turtles
Lizards
Green Iguanas and Other Iguanids
Reptile and Amphibian Parasites
Newts
Snakes
Tarantulas and Scorpions
Chameleons
Tortoises

Publisher's Note: All of the photographs in this book have been coated with FOTOGLAZE™ finish, a special lamination that imparts new dimension of colorful gloss to the photographs.

Reinforced Library Binding & Super-Highest Quality Boards

This edition ©1994 TFH Publications, Inc., 1 TFH Plaza, Neptune Ci NJ 07753. This special library bound edition is made expressly for Chelsea House Publishers, a division of Main Line Book Company.

Library of Congress Cataloging-in-Publication Data

Schmidt, W. (Wolfgang).
    Chameleon care and breeding/ W. Schmidt, K. Tamm, E. Wallikewitz.
    p. cm. — (Reptiles and amphibians)
    Includes index.
    Summary: Discusses the natural history, care, and breeding of chameleons.
    ISBN 0-7910-5082-3 (hc: alk. paper)
    1. Chameleons as pets—Juvenile literature. 2. Chameleons—   Juvenile literature
Chameleons—Breeding—Juvenile literature. I. Tamm, K. (Klaus) II. Wallikewitz, E. (Erich)
Title. IV. Series.
        SF459.C45S36 1998
        639.3'95—dc21   98-19050
                                                         CIP
                                                         AC

VOLUME 2

Because of today's increasing nvironmental destruction and urbanization, many people want to ring a bit of nature nto their homes. ncreasngly the method of choice is he errarium. The ascinating chamelons call o mind dragons or dinosaurs and often are found on the wish lists of hobbyists. Unfortunately, only a few publications on keeping and breeding chameleons exist in the popular literature, and often potential hobbyists are informed hat chameleons cannot be kept successfully in captivity. Only recently has captive-bred stock started to appear on dealer lists and n pet shops, making it possible for serious hobbyists to begin to consider chameleons as pets worth heir investment in time and money.

The many peculiarities of chameleons, which extend far beyond their ability to change color and the "shooting tongue trick," are often unknown even to interested amateur herpetologists. This book, Volume 2, presents the fascinating world of chameleons, ancient but

R. ZOBEL

A beautiful color variety of *Chamaeleo pardalis*, the Panther Chameleon, from St. Marie.

very specialized lizards that have managed to survive into modern times. Beyond that, it is meant to provide guidance in setting up and maintaining terraria and in solving problems that come up. Special emphasis in this book has been placed on terrarium technology, because technology is the reason for greater breeding successes in captivity.

These books make no claim to completeness, but rather are only intended to provide an overview of the commonly kept chameleon species and to familiarize the reader with these widely known, but in detail still quite unknown, dragons of our time. Volume 1 deals with species descriptions.

Originally published in German under the title *CHÄMALEONS Drachen unserer Zeit* by Terrarien Bibliothek. Copyright 1989 by Herpetologischer Fachverlag.

WHAT IS A CHAMELEON?

REMARKS ON TAXONOMY

When they see the word taxonomy, some readers will be alarmed and will pass over this chapter. Nevertheless, we believe that for the interested hobbyist it is necessary to deal with this subject in order to have a better understanding of just what type of animals chameleons are and where they stand in relation to the rest of the lizards.

The class Reptilia consists of four orders. Of these, however, we are only interested in the order of the lizards and snakes, Squamata. This order includes the suborder Sauria (the lizards), to which the family Chamaeleonidae belongs. Chameleons are very closely related to both the iguanin lizards (anoles, iguanas, and their relatives) and the agamids (agamas, bearded dragons, mastigures, etc.), and some recent papers have even questioned whether these groups should all be distinct families. The division of the Chamaeleonidae into genera, species, and subspecies also is in a state of flux, so a brief historic

A gravid female *Chamaeleo labordi* displaying a color pattern used to repel an approaching male.

R. D. BARTLETT

R. D. BARTLETT

A red-phase female Panther Chameleon, *Chamaeleo pardalis*. Colors are used by chameleons for communication, every mood and aspect of the life history being represented by subtly different colors and patterns.

overview is in order here.

In his 1902 publication "Prodomus einer Monographie der Chamäleonten," Werner proposed that the chameleons comprised three genera, namely *Chamaeleo, Brookesia,* and *Rhampholeon.* The true chameleons belonged to the genus *Chamaeleo.* The representatives of the genera *Brookesia* and *Rhampholeon* were the stub-tailed or dwarf chameleons, often called the ground chameleons because of their preference for low shrubs. He distinguished a total of 70 species, later recognizing 88 species in his expanded list of 1911. In 1959 Hillenius published a classification that contained only 69 species. Mertens (1966), with 84 species, and Schifter (1971), with 86 species, even decreased the number of genera to two, *Brookesia* and *Chamaeleo.*

Most recently, Klaver and Boehme (1986) have taken on the difficult task of determining the natural kinship of the species, which is reflected in their systematics. They studied two important morphological characters, the hemipenis and the lung, in about 70 percent of the chameleon species and came

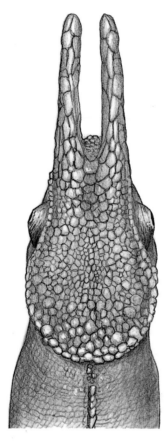

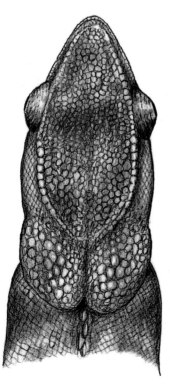

to the following conclusion:

The family Chamaeleonidae is divided into two subfamilies, Chamaeleoninae (true chameleons) and Brookesiinae (ground chameleons—stub-tailed and leaf chameleons). The first subfamily contains four genera:

Calumma (for example, *Calumma brevicornis*); *Furcifer* (for example, *Furcifer lateralis*); *Bradypodion* (for example, *Bradypodion fischeri*); *Chamaeleo* (for example, *Chamaeleo chamaeleon*).

The genus *Chamaeleo* is divided further into the subgenera *Chamaeleo* and *Triocerus* (the horned chameleons, such as *Chamaeleo (Triocerus) jacksonii*).

The subfamily Brookesiinae, in contrast, has only two genera:

Brookesia (Madagascan ground or dwarf chameleons, for example, *Brookesia stumpffi*) and *Rhampholeon* (African ground or leaf chameleons, for example, *Rhampholeon brevicaudatus*).

(Note to the English-language edition: Readers should keep in mind that this classification is not accepted by all workers in the field of lizard taxonomy and has been challenged by some very competent scientists. Recent work on the morphology and cellular chemistry of the chameleons

Top Left: A Madagascan chameleon with two long scale-covered horns in the male, *Chamaeleo bifidus*. Art by J. R. Quinn, based on Brygoo, 1971. **Bottom Left:** Movable nape flaps are a feature of *Chamaeleo dilepis*, the Flap-necked Chameleon. Art by J. R. Quinn, based on Witte, 1965.

seems to show that at least the genera *Calumma* and *Furcifer* contain species that are not closely related to the type species of the genera, thus making the genera as defined by Klaver and Boehme paraphyletic or artificial. See Rieppel, Walker, and Odhiambo, 1992, *Journal of Herpetology*, 26(1): 77-80, for a brief survey of the problem and a listing of some of the more recent

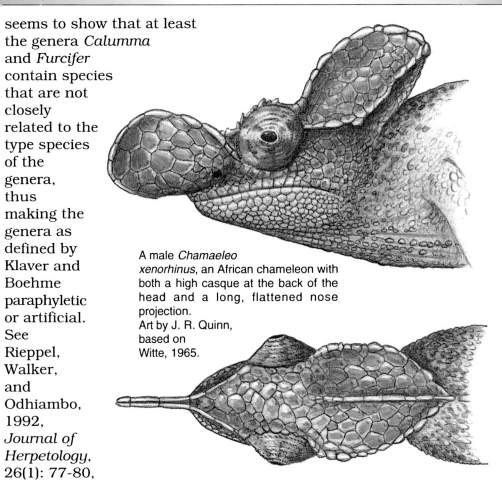

A male *Chamaeleo xenorhinus*, an African chameleon with both a high casque at the back of the head and a long, flattened nose projection.
Art by J. R. Quinn, based on Witte, 1965.

literature. See also Frost and Etheridge, 1989, *Misc. Publications Univ. Kansas Museum Nat. Hist.*, No. 81: 65 pages, for a recent and controversial discussion of relationships of the chameleons and agamids; this paper was reviewed in a more readable version by Walls, 1991, *Tropical Fish Hobbyist*, 40(4): 116/128. Additionally, the large chameleons of Madagascar have relatives in Africa and possibly represent at least two separate lines of evolution.

In keeping with this more questioning attitude toward the taxonomy of the chameleons, this English-language edition recognizes only four genera of living chameleons: a broad genus *Chamaeleo*, to include *Chamaeleo* proper plus *Calumma* and *Furcifer* as used by Klaver and Boehme, for larger chameleons with complex lungs and a narrow parietal bone in the skull, usually oviparous; *Bradypodion*, for the southern African dwarf chameleons, with simple lungs, a narrow parietal bone, and usually

(?always) livebearing; *Brookesia*, to include the Madagascan dwarf or ground chameleons, of tiny size—less than 12 cm, 5 inches—and with fairly short, weakly prehensile tails; and *Rhampholeon,* including the African leaf or ground chameleons, of tiny size, often very high-bodied, and with short, stumpy tails. *Chamaeleo* and *Bradypodion* seem to be very closely related, while *Brookesia* and *Rhampholeon* often are considered synonyms, though the large Madagascar chameleons possibly are more closely related to *Rhampholeon* than to most African *Chamaeleo*. The taxonomy of the genera of chameleons is sure to change in the future, so the hobbyist should not be too upset if unusual names and combinations are found in the literature.)

R. ZOBEL

A large chameleon, like this Panther Chameleon, *Chamaeleo pardalis*, can inflict a serious bite if given a chance. Don't be deceived by the odd appearance of these lizards—they are very aggressive.

CHAMELEONS, MODERN DRAGONS

The Chamaeleonidae are vertebrates belonging to the class Reptilia and, within the class, to the lizard group, Squamata. The Squamata appeared about 195 million years ago in the Triassic. Within it in the course of time evolved the family Chamaeleonidae, which is about 100 million years old and goes back to the Cretaceous. The area of occurrence must formerly have been considerably larger, for fossil remains have even been discovered in Bavaria. Today only relic populations exist in Europe in the Mediterranean region.

The chameleons are highly variable. The greatest differences are found between the two subfamilies. The Chamaeleoninae are usually large (up to 80 centimeters, 32 inches, in total length) and colorful animals. In contrast, the Brookesiinae are usually tiny, plain gray or brown animals. The smallest known species is *Brookesia minima*, with a maximum total length of 34 millimeters (1.5 inches).

In several chameleon species the animals have such a different appearance depending on age and sex that it is very difficult for the average hobbyist to know for sure to what species they belong. Among their most impressive characters are the head ornaments of some chameleons. In many species there is a bony frill or casque at the nape (occiput) of the head that may be covered with large scales and flexible only near the center. There are species with one, two, three, four, or six horns. Other species have developed horny snout (rostral) processes that give them an imposing appearance. Still others have colored folds of skin on the throat (gular pouches or folds) that they can spread so the lizard looks larger and can scare off predators. This can be very impressive, as when you try to grab a chameleon. Though it may be hard to detect in its habitat and makes no attempt to escape, when touched it spreads the folds of skin on the throat and with wide-open mouth attacks the hand while hissing loudly. In *Chamaeleo dilepis* and a few other species the flaps of skin behind the head are flexible. When attacked, these chameleons spread the flaps like the ears of an elephant, creating quite an impressive show. Opinions differ on the significance of the horns and snout processes, though it is certain that the males use them in ritual fighting. Moreover, Boehme and Klaver (1981) showed with the Cameroon mountain species that they can also play a role in species recognition.

For a long time the scientific community assumed that the family Chamaeleonidae evolved on the island of Madagascar (because there are so many species there), but it is thought today that the chameleons actually originated in East Africa. From there they colonized all of Africa, the Mediterranean region, the Arabian Peninsula, India, and Sri Lanka. The centers of occurrence are East Africa, West Africa (especially Cameroon), and Madagascar. Today the majority of the approximately 120 species of Chamaeleoninae and approximately 30 Brookesiinae species live on Madagascar, where they were able to reach their greatest diversity.

FIRST-CLASS CLIMBING ARTISTS

The chameleons are lizards that are best adapted to life in trees and bushes. For this purpose

Parson's Chameleon, *Chamaeleo parsoni*, is among the largest lizards, with some specimens reaching 50 cm, 20 inches. It also is a very bulky animal.

W. SCHMIDT

they are equipped with modified gripping feet, a prehensile tail, independently movable eyes, and a projectile tongue. At airy heights, well-camouflaged in the surrounding foliage, the animals spend most of the day hunting from ambush, always on the watch for approaching insects, which they catch with the aid of their strangely modified tongue.

Most chameleons love sunlight; only a few extreme forest-dwellers (for example, most dwarf chameleons) avoid the sun. In contrast to the true chameleons, the dwarf chameleons from Madagascar have evolved into forest-dwellers that avoid all sunlight and are found only in the leaves of shrubs in the forest understory. They spend the day searching through the leaves for food, and thanks to their good camouflage they are virtually impossible to detect there. The African leaf chameleons also live in the leaves of low forest shrubs. A few species have additionally exploited the savannahs as a living space, where they are found in tussocks of grass near the ground. In addition, a few species of true chameleons have also evolved back into ground-dwellers. These species include *Chamaeleo namaquensis* from Namibia and South Africa and *Chamaeleo chamaeleon* from the southern Algerian Sahara, where it inhabits sand dunes and oases.

Chameleons live in all vegetation zones, from the desert to the rainforest, and each species within these zones of vegetation inhabits a specific

A gravid female *Chamaeleo minor*. Gravid females often have the most brilliant colors. Photo: R. D. Bartlett.

living space. From this it is easy to see how hard it is to know how to keep a Flap-necked Chameleon (*Chamaeleo dilepis*), for example, under the appropriate conditions. This species inhabits virtually all of Africa south of the Sahara. The care of the Flap-necked Chameleon is possible only when the precise source of the specimens is known and information can be found about which type of biotope the lizards inhabited. On the other hand, imagine the surprise of the mountain climber who ascends Mount Kenya and at an altitude of 4500 meters (14850 feet), right at the snow line, encounters a chameleon. This species is *Chamaeleo schubotzi*, the chameleon with the widest distribution in elevation. It would thus be highly advantageous to collect the animals yourself, in the course of which you could observe their habits in the wild, but obviously this is not even feasible for most hobbyists. Additionally, rampant collecting of delicate and poorly known animals such as chameleons cannot be recommended and is likely to be against the law in most areas. The hobbyist is much better off trying a captive-bred specimen before dealing with expensive wild-caught animals.

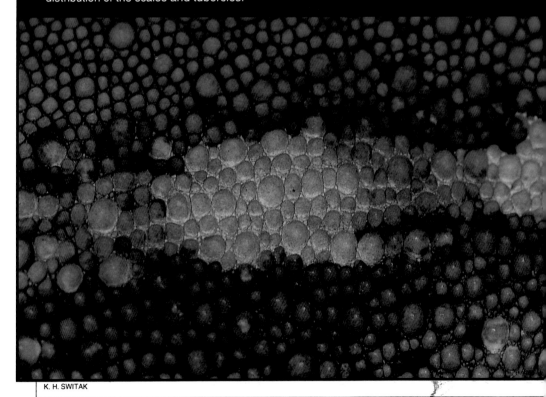

A close-up of the skin of a Veiled Chameleon, *Chamaeleo calyptratus*, shows the presence of two different sizes of scales or tubercles. Often chameleon identification is based in part on the size and distribution of the scales and tubercles.

K. H. SWITAK

E. RICEPUTI

Panther Chameleons, *Chamaeleo pardalis*, are among the most commonly seen chameleons, with many available specimens being captive-bred. Notice the pale lip stripe, broken pale midbody stripe, and finely serrated crest on the back.

Captive-bred chameleons come from a known biotope—the terrarium—that can be readily duplicated.

MASTERS OF CAMOUFLAGE

To find a chameleon in its natural living space takes persistence and patience because chameleons are masters of camouflage! With their flattened bodies and green to brown coloration they mimic almost perfectly objects in their immediate vicinity: living or dead leaves, branches, and tufts of grass. This makes them very hard to detect in their living space, not only by people but by their predators as well. All true chameleons have in common that the body form, corresponding to their arboreal habits, is leaf-shaped. The leaf chameleons go the true chameleons one better in that they imitate living leaves swaying in the wind: they move in jerky steps, always a short distance forward and a shorter distance back, so that the chameleons are no longer conspicuous as a static point. Some chameleons always display this behavior whenever they are disturbed or they feel they are being observed. This is most pronounced in juveniles.

In the ground chameleons mimicry is much more developed than in the true chameleons. This is probably also the reason why they are so seldom seen. Formerly it was simply claimed that the *Brookesia* species with their dorsal serrations were branch mimics and the *Rhampholeon* species were leaf mimics. This generalization, however, is simply not true. When you observe a *Brookesia stumpffi*, it calls to mind a withered leaf more than it does a branch. The mimicry is strengthened when the animals freeze when approached and sometimes even close their eyes. Other forms of mimicry are also found in the African ground chameleons, such as the grass mimicry of *Rhampholeon kerstenii* described by Friederich (1985).

The ground chameleons have evolved yet another peculiarity: akinesis (playing possum). A chameleon lying motionless as if dead is no longer recognized as prey by a predator and hence has a good chance to survive. This behavior is always played out in the same way. It is triggered by touching the animal or by shaking the object on which the ground chameleon is resting. The animal tucks in its legs, stiffens its body, and lets itself fall to the ground, where it lies motionless. Some ground chameleons (several *Brookesia* species) have skeletons of extremely complicated

Bradypodion karroicum is a dwarf chameleon often found in Karroo National Park in South Africa, where it inhabits thorn scrub. Identification of South African dwarf chameleons is complicated because they are so variable and have very small ranges.

K. H. SWITAK

R. S. SIMMONS

The Mountain Chameleon, *Chamaeleo montium*, from the higher elevations of the Cameroons in western Africa may be very abundant locally. Males have not only horns but high crests on the back and tail.

structure that help protect them from, for example, the bills of birds that might want to test whether something edible has fallen to the ground. These species have a framework of accessory ribs over the backbone that gives extraordinary protection to the spinal cord and deflects the thrusts of the bills, so that the ground chameleons do not have to give up their state of akinesis. In this connection it should be mentioned that the ground chameleons possess ossified endolymphic sacs that form a supplementary balance organ, with the aid of which they can always maneuver themselves into the prone position (Boehme, 1982; Schmidt, Henkel, and Boehme, 1989).

In conclusion, it can be said that chameleons, through their combination of structural and behavioral mimicry—true chameleons resembling living leaves swaying in the wind, ground chameleons mimicking dry leaves, branches, or tufts of grass and employing akinesis—are almost perfectly adapted to their natural environment. This is part of the explanation for how these usually slow and seemingly defenseless animals have been able to survive until today.

GENERAL BIOLOGY

TEMPERATURE REGULATION

Like all reptiles, chameleons are cold-blooded. They thus are unable to maintain a constant body temperature like mammals and birds, but rather are dependent on the ambient temperature. This is one of the reasons that chameleons only inhabit the warmer regions.

To regulate their temperature—that is, to reach the preferred temperature and to guard against overheating—chameleons have evolved several strategies. In the morning and on cool days chameleons are dark in color so as to be able to absorb all of the heat radiation from the sun. To exploit the sun's radiation even more intensively, chameleons flatten their body so that they can expose the largest possible surface area to the sun. When the animals are warm they always turn a lighter color—some species even turn almost white—to reflect as much of the heat radiation as possible. If the temperature rises further, chameleons seek out protection from the sun in the shade. If even this is not enough, they try to cool

Madagascar has a tremendous diversity of chameleons, often with very specialized habitat requirements. The tiny species of ground chameleons, like this *Brookesia ebenaui*, often die when not allowed to escape to the coolness of their burrows.

R. D. BARTLETT

R. D. BARTLETT

Still commonly imported but now also sometimes captive-bred, the spectacular Jackson's Chameleon, *Chamaeleo jacksonii*, survives well in a greenhouse. This is a male of the form found in the Meru Mountains, Tanzania.

themselves through evaporation by opening their mouth. Extra caution is recommended with juveniles, because they cannot yet regulate their temperature well and their small bodies overheat quickly.

MOLTING

The epidermis is made up of very horny scales that can vary in size, number, and form depending on the species. In chameleons the following kinds of scales are distinguished: granular scales, tubercular scales, laminar scales, conical scales, and keeled scales. Because the epidermis consists of dead keratin cells, it does not grow along with the rest of the body and must be replaced in the molt (or shed) at regular intervals. For this reason juveniles molt quite frequently then always more infrequently with advancing age. At the start of the molt the skin takes on a dull, milky appearance, then it usually loosens in shreds. Chameleons assist this process by rubbing themselves against branches and rocks. In addition, with the aid of the mouth and feet they try to pull off the remaining skin. After the molt they again exhibit the most beautiful colors. The duration of the shed varies depending on the species. Some need hours, others days.

This gravid female Veiled Chameleon, *Chamaeleo calyptratus*, shows the modifications of the feet typical of chameleons, the toes fused and covered with skin to produce excellent branch graspers.

R. D. BARTLETT

LIMBS

Chameleons are distinguished by many peculiar anatomical characteristics, most of which are adaptations to the arboreal living space. For example, in all chameleons the feet, through the fusion of two and three toes into separate clasping digits on each foot, have been transformed into functional tongs with which the chameleons can cling to branches extremely well. Furthermore, in the true chameleons the long tail is very flexible and equipped with rough scales on the underside so that it serves as the ideal prehensile tail for anchoring to branches. The ground chameleons are not able to use their tail very well for clasping; only the tip of the tail is somewhat mobile and is used for support.

Chameleons are not able to regenerate the tail or other body parts. Therefore, animals with healed wounds and short, defective tails often are found in the wild. The other peculiar characters of chameleons will be discussed separately in the following sections.

SHARP-EYED HUNTERS WITH A PANORAMIC VIEW

With their specially constructed conical eyes, chameleons enjoy a 360° field of view. The eyes can be moved independently of each other, so a chameleon can simultaneously look to the front and the rear. This panoramic view enables the chameleons to inspect their whole surroundings without revealing their position through movements, such as the turning of the head. Particularly noteworthy is the fact that the proportionately arge, conical eye of the chameleon protrudes far out from the head and in comparison to other reptiles has substantially greater freedom of movement. This furnishes the chameleon a 180° horizontal and a 90° vertical field of view for each eye, so a chameleon really can view its world in all directions without moving its head.

In the search for food the eyes roam restlessly until a prey animal is detected by its movement. Then both eyes are fixed on the animal until it is within favorable shooting range. Binocular vision is advantageous for judging distance. It is based on the circumstance that through lateral separation of the eyes two different images are created. The slight difference is evaluated by the brain, which combines the two images into one to estimate the distance.

Like almost all vertebrates, chameleons have eyes with movable lenses, which is universally recognized as the most highly developed type of eye. The lids of each eye have fused into a hemisphere, but a hole remains open in the middle to allow light to enter the pupil. Because the lids are attached to the eyeball, they join in practically all of its movements. When the chameleon returns to its roost to sleep, the hole in the lid is closed and the eyeball turns downward. In this matter the pupil comes to rest behind a bony lamina, which blocks out every ray of light.

The chameleon eye with both its eyelid opening and the pupil thus possesses a double aperture. The eyelid hole acts as a second shutter and apparently increases accuracy when the eyes are locked

The eyes of chameleons, like this *Chamaeleo balteatus*, are in turrets of fused skin and can be moved independently in a broad arc.

Head horns of various types, usually scale-covered extensions of the snout or casque, are common in male chameleons, where they probably serve both to impress females and in ritual fights between males. The large projection on this male *Chamaeleo fischeri*, Fischer's Chameleon, is fairly typical of many species.

on the prey with binocular vision. However, the intensity of light is decreased in this way.

Observations show that chameleons need good lighting conditions to make accurate tongue shots, and furthermore that the animals, when kept in inadequate illumination, "misfire" a surprisingly high percentage of the time—the tongue always falls short of the target. When the tongue is catapulted, the eyes are closed when the prey is pulled in to help avoid eye injuries. Sometimes the eye of a chameleon is pushed almost completely out of the head and the eyeball is moved under the eyelids. This always happens when the animal wants to expel a foreign body or rubs itself against a branch to scrape off dead skin during the molt. The hobbyist seeing this for the first time will surely get a scare, because it appears as if the eye were going to pop completely out of the head.

THE TRICK WITH THE CATAPULT TONGUE

The same situation arises again and again: visitors look at a chameleon and suddenly, like a blur to the unprepared eye, an insect disappears into the animal's mouth. With a somewhat confused expression, the visitor asks the hobbyist: What happened?

The visitor has experienced one of the most unusual methods of catching prey that the animal world can offer. Chameleons are able to shoot out their tongue, catch a prey animal, and draw it back into the mouth along with the tongue. A brilliant "tongue trick"! Of course, not every shot is on the mark. Factors such as brightness, temperature, and the speed of the prey play a role (Schuster, 1979).

The functional principle of the chameleon tongue was unclear for a long time. In 1828, J. Houston theorized that an increase in blood pressure, similar to that causing erection of the penis in reptiles and mammals, was responsible for the catapulting of the tongue. Later opinions changed with advances in knowledge, until Altevogt and Altevogt published their "Studien zur Kinematik der Chamäleonzunge" ("Studies of the kinematics of the chameleon tongue"), upon which we draw heavily in the following discussion. The

chameleon tongue is about as long as the body, in some species even longer. At its tip is located a clublike thickening. At the tip of this club is a bowl-like depression that is equipped with glands. These secrete a sticky substance (Altevogt and Altevogt, 1954). With the aid of the hyoid bone (a slender bone in the base of the tongue of most reptiles) and various longitudinal and circular muscles, the tongue is catapulted out and retracted again.

The process of prey capture can be divided into five phases:

Phase 1: First, both eyes lock onto an insect (*aiming*).

Phase 2: The animal opens the mouth and pushes the tongue forward slightly, so that the

The early phases of the "trick with the catapult tongue" as displayed by the Knysna Dwarf Chameleon, *Bradypodion damarana*. The eyes first are locked on the prey, and then the tongue is pushed forward slowly from the partially open mouth. Males of this little chameleon are very colorful, including bright blue on the head, while females are mottled. Photos: G. Dingerkus.

clublike tip becomes visible. This state can be maintained for up to four seconds (*protrusion*).

Phase 3: Now the animal "shoots" the tongue out and clasps the prey animal with the tip of the tongue (*projection*). The insect is also held tight by the stickiness of a secretion. Altevogt and Altevogt give for this phase in *Chamaeleo chamaeleon* a time of 0.039 to 0.54 second at a distance of 15 centimeters (6 inches) to the prey animal.

Phase 4: The drawing in of the tongue with the prey (*retraction*) now occurs four to five times more slowly than the shooting phase. The rate is influenced by the weight of the prey animal. In this process the clublike end of the tongue always swings downward.

Phase 5: The prey is chewed and swallowed. Even if the chameleon has missed its prey, a swallowing movement still always occurs.

It is a mistake, however, to assume that chameleons have to use their tongue in the manner described above to capture a prey animal. Food animals such as slugs, those that cannot be taken in with the tongue, and prey that is very close are also occasionally seized with the jaws alone, without "shooting" (Altevogt and Altevogt, 1954).

The performance of the chameleon tongue has also been studied. Dischner (1958) used a 100-gram spring balance to which he attached food animals. Then he let two *Chamaeleo montium* "shoot" at these animals. In his paper he cites 43 grams as the maximum value of the pulling power of the

The Madagascan *Chamaeleo oshaughnessyi*. Notice the lack of a crest under the throat and the large tubercles on the limbs and lower sides.

R. D. BARTLETT

Chameleons may be very difficult to identify. This specimen has been called *Chamaeleo quadricornis*. Notice the low crest at the base of the tail similar to that of the Mountain Chameleon.

tongue. Larger chameleons, however, certainly must be even more powerful.

Parcher (1974) was the first to describe a behavior of chameleons that formerly had been known only of other lizards (for example, *Anolis*). The chameleon sticks its tongue slightly out of its mouth and touches the tip to the ground or branch just in front of it. We have observed this behavior in all chameleons that we have kept in the terrarium. The probability is thus very high that the other species also have this ability. Schwenk (1985) found taste buds when he studied the tongue of *Chamaeleo jacksonii*. Because chameleons have a degenerative Jacobson's organ (one of the organs of smell), he concluded that the sense of taste is more significant in chameleons than is the sense of smell.

THE PLAY OF COLORS AS A SUBSTITUTE FOR LANGUAGE

The ability of chameleons to change color is universally known. Chameleons, for example, can "blacken with rage." It is commonly assumed that the chameleon matches its coloration to its surroundings so as to avoid detection. Anyone who has the opportunity, however, to observe chameleons for a fairly long time will soon notice that the change in color is principally of a physiological nature: the chameleon expresses its mood through its color, responding to conspecifics as well as the environment. The coloration and the change in color are thus essentially an instrument of communication that often is accompanied by specific behavior patterns, such as the flattening of the body, nodding of the head, or the up-and-down wagging of the whole body.

It is not true that all chameleons can turn any color they please. The spectrum of colors at their disposal varies from species to species. Besides the species-specific palette of colors, the coloration is also dependent on other factors. First and foremost is the general physical condition. Sick or weakened animals often are pale in color. In contrast, a healthy, robust animal will normally display rich, bright colors. In excited animals these colors often become garish and are considerably richer in contrast than when the animals are calm. Visual contact with conspecifics, particularly from male to male, almost always leads to agitation in the animals. If an animal is permanently aroused, sooner or later it exhibits a special stress coloration over its whole body, usually a conspicuously dark shade and in extreme cases even black. If the stress factor is not removed, it can lead to the death of the chameleon. The remaining environmental influences like time of day, light intensity, and temperature also strongly influence the coloration of chameleons. For example, the body markings are far more intense in bright sunlight than at night or when the chameleon is resting.

But what is responsible for the change in color in chameleons in the first place? For a long time the mechanism of this fascinating process was unknown, and many

Chamaeleo verrucosa, one of the many larger chameleons of Madagascar currently being imported for the hobby market. Notice the large tubercles in a line on the midside and the smaller tubercles in oblique rows on the upper side.

R. D. BARTLETT

more or less erroneous theories were proposed. Today it is certain that the change in color is caused by the migration of a dark pigment, called melanin, from deeper skin layers to layers nearer the surface. This pigment migrates within the pigment cells, the melanophores. If it spreads throughout the entire cell, the coloration looks darker; if it coalesces at a point in the cell, lighter shades result.

The ground color of a chameleon is produced by the pigment cells, the chromatophores, present in the upper layers of skin. They are located above the melanophores and generally are shades of yellow and red. True blue and green pigments are not available at all in reptiles. These colors are produced by another sort of color cell, the guanophores. They contain a semicrystalline substance called guanine. This guanine is actually colorless, but acts as a reflector and thereby changes in a decisive manner the incident light. Through the scattering of light of specific wavelengths the color blue is produced. If a layer of yellow chromatophores is located above the guanophores, the color green, so widely distributed in reptiles, is produced. The coloration of a chameleon thus is influenced by a complex interplay of the pigment cells with the cells containing melanin, which produce the changing colors through the overlying layer of chromatophores.

The movement of the melanin in the melanophores is controlled by energy from the nervous system. This explains why sick or weak

R. D. BARTLETT

It is likely that intensified colors, as on the eyes of this male Parson's Chameleon, *Chamaeleo parsoni*, all have a meaning to other chameleons.

animals turn pale. They lack the strength to produce the energy needed to distribute the melanin inside the cells. Experiments have shown that injuries to the spinal cord of a chameleon cause the skin behind the injury to darken and to lose the ability to lighten.

DRAGONS NEED OFFSPRING, TOO

EGGS AND LIVE BIRTH

To care for terrarium animals so that they also breed is one of the most difficult tasks. For a long time chameleons were considered to be particularly problematic animals, but in recent years there have been some successes. Species such as the Carpet Chameleon (*Chamaeleo lateralis*), Veiled Chameleon (*Chamaeleo calyptratus*), Helmeted Chameleon (*Chamaeleo hoehnelii*), Cape Dwarf Chameleon (*Bradypodion pumilum*), and Jackson's Chameleon (*Chamaeleo jacksonii*) are bred with some frequency today though seldom on a commercial scale.

At this point we would like to discuss a few general topics. In chameleons three kinds of reproduction are currently known: 1) ovipary (egg-laying); 2) ovovivipary (livebearing); 3) parthenogenesis (asexual reproduction).

Ovipary is the most widely distributed of the types of reproduction. Fertilized eggs are

laid in self-excavated nest burrows or depressions. The female usually lays the eggs three to six weeks after copulation. Before she lays the eggs she searches for a suitable laying site. If one is not found right away, she can continue to hold the eggs in her body for a while. Nevertheless, the time of egg-laying cannot be delayed forever. Females that cannot find a good site or are weakened can suffer from egg-binding. When the female chameleon has found a suitable laying place, she digs a hole into which she disappears. After the eggs are laid, the nest hole is carefully filled in. With that the chameleon's job is finished.

Like some other reptiles, the females of several chameleon species are able to store sperm in their bodies. In this way they are able, without additional copulation, to lay fertilized eggs one to several more times. The advantage of this method with animals as solitary as chameleons should be obvious to everyone.

After eggs have been

The gorgeous Panther Chameleon, *Chamaeleo pardalis*, lays eggs, like most other chameleons. Incubating the eggs can be a major undertaking, however, that will tax the abilities of even the most experienced hobbyist. Photo: M. Panzella.

laid successfully in the terrarium, they should be removed from the substrate and placed in an incubator. Otherwise there is the danger that the eggs could be damaged.

The egg itself consists of an embryo surrounded by the amnion, a large supply of yolk with a yolk membrane, the allantois for the storage of metabolic waste products, and the chorion directly under the porous, parchmentlike shell. Later the chorion and allantois combine into the chorio-allantois, which takes in oxygen through the shell and releases carbon dioxide. The development from fertilization of the oocyte to the hatching of the young chameleon is called embryonic development. During this time the embryo consumes the entire yolk supply. With the aid of the egg tooth on the tip of the snout the ready-to-hatch youngster opens the shell. Later the egg tooth is simply shed, leaving no evidence of this curious "tool."

In several species, such as *Chamaeleo montium*, hatching is announced by the shrinking and "sweating" of the egg. Normally a few hours later the little chameleon will stick the tip of its snout out of the egg to breathe.

The most difficult problem is the selection of the proper incubation temperature. Based on our findings, temperatures between 20°C and 28°C (68 to 82°F) should be considered the most favorable. Nevertheless, it should be mentioned that the embryo may require a rest period. An example of this is offered by the Carpet

Chameleon (*Chamaeleo lateralis*). The sex ratio of the offspring is dependent on the temperature during development.

Possibly the most fascinating type of reproduction is found in the livebearing (ovoviviparous) chameleons. Strictly speaking, the term "livebearing" is incorrect, because the embryo is not nourished by the mother's blood stream through a placenta. A calcium-free membrane (not really an egg shell) surrounds the embryo during its entire development in the oviduct. The female waits to lay the shell-less eggs until just before they hatch, and the youngsters free themselves from the membrane very quickly. Hence there is no incubation period in ovoviviparous species, but rather only a gestation period. On average, gestation lasts three to six months. The "livebearing" chameleon species also practice sperm storage. Atsatt (1953) was able to demonstrate this for the first time in chameleons with *Bradypodion pumilum*.

An extremely unusual form of reproduction, which so far has been observed in only one species of the family Chamaeleonidae, is shown by *Rhampholeon boulengeri*, which reproduces by parthenogenesis. The female reproduces offspring from unfertilized eggs without requiring sperm. Unfortunately, detailed

information is lacking on this interesting species.

SEX DIFFERENCES

Probably the goal of all hobbyists is to breed the animals they keep. An important prerequisite for breeding is to know the sex of the animals under your care. As a rule, the sexes of chameleons are very easy to distinguish. The base of the tail as seen from the side and above is clearly thicker in the male than in the female. In some dwarf chameleons the sex is easier to distinguish from above than from the side. With the small species a magnifying glass must be used. Other possible distinguishing characters include the differently colored membrane of the throat sac (gular pouch), body size, coloration, and head ornamentation. In some chameleon species the males possess conspicuous heel spurs.

EGG INCUBATION AND REARING

The successful incubation of chameleon eggs laid in the terrarium has unfortunately been the exception so far (as opposed to mating and egg-laying in the greenhouse or other outdoor situations). We are aware of only two cases of successful egg incubation, by Henkel with *Brookesia stumpffi* eggs and by Mueller with *Chamaeleo dilepis* eggs. We have only managed to incubate the eggs of *Brookesia minima* in the terrarium. The two species of ground chameleon do not require high temperatures for incubation. Besides the risk of losing eggs due to improper conditions, there is also the danger

Left: *Chamaeleo antimena* is an uncommon Madagascan chameleon. This specimen, probably a young male, does not have a fully developed dorsal crest as yet, but it shows the bright white stripe down the center of the belly typical of the species. Photo: P. Freed.

that the soft-shelled eggs will fall prey to the food insects. Therefore, the eggs should be removed from the terrarium immediately after they are laid. When removing the eggs it is essential to make sure that their orientation is not changed. The precise time when the embryo becomes attached to the top side of the shell varies from species to species. With some species, such as *Chamaeleo lateralis* and *Chamaeleo campani,* the embryonic disc is clearly visible as a small red circle. This indicates that the egg is certainly fertilized. In most species, however, the embryonic disc is not visible.

The only substrates we recommend for incubation are vermiculite and perlite. These are small mineral chips that do a great job of absorbing and holding water, so the eggs can absorb water without being in direct contact with it. The eggs of a few chameleon species are very sensitive to drops of water or too much dampness. Others are completely insensitive and can even be sprayed to moisten the substrate. Only the bottom half of the egg takes up water; the top half serves exclusively for the exchange of gases. Therefore, it is best to bury the eggs halfway in the incubation substrate. The substrate must always be kept slightly moist. For most species the substrate contains the correct amount of moisture when water no longer runs from it, it holds together slightly, and when the water runs out between the fingers when the substrate is squeezed. It has proved to be beneficial to moisten

the substrate, when necessary, about every three weeks by spraying the rim of the container. All tightly closing plastic containers with transparent covers (such as refrigerator food-storage containers) are suitable for maturing eggs. Regular testing of the dampness of the medium also ensures adequate gas exchange. You can build your own incubator according to the specifications given in books on reptile breeding. The eggs of some chameleons do not need an incubator because they do not need constant temperatures. For example, the

eggs of *Chamaeleo dilepis* can be brought to maturity easily with daytime temperatures of 30°C (86°F) and normal room temperatures at night.

The eggs of ground chameleons are best matured only at room temperature, because they are very sensitive to high temperatures. Other special requirements are given in the species descriptions. For the incubation of the eggs of chameleon species that are not presented in the species descriptions, we recommend a thorough study of the climate of the natural habitat to determine the preferred incubation temperature. In general, for rainforest dwellers the temperature should not be too high. A temperature range of 18 to a maximum of 25°C (65 to 77°F) is suitable.

Just before hatching, the egg begins to shrink and sweat. Later the youngster cuts a star-shaped opening on one side and sticks its head out. The hatchling usually spends several hours in this position.

When the adult animals have been well cared for and have received adequate amounts of calcium and vitamins, and when the eggs have been incubated properly, rearing of the offspring presents no problems. Even minor negligence during pregnancy can cause the young not to hatch or to grow poorly or not at all. For the care of the offspring virtually the same applies as for that of the adults. The youngsters are kept singly in small containers. Do not try to raise more than one chamaeleon in a container, because the aggressiveness in some species is even greater in the juvenile stage. Even in less territorial species the dominant male would oppress all of the others and would prevent the expression of the sex-specific characters in the other males. In the rearing enclosure the ventilation surfaces should be

Left: From Tanzania comes the seldom-seen *Chamaeleo deremensis*, one of the horned species that also has a high dorsal crest in both sexes. Photo: P.· Freed.

Above: A hatchling *Chamaeleo jacksonii xantholophus*, the subspecies typical of Mt. Kenya and Mt. Meru. Tiny chameleons require lots of small insect food, including flies attracted to ripe fruit. Photo: R. D. Bartlett. **Below:** The Cape Dwarf Chameleon, *Bradypodion pumilum*, is restricted to the southwestern Cape region of South Africa. This juvenile might have 20 or more brothers and sisters produced by its mother in one year. Photo: P. Freed.

larger than in the terraria for the adult animals. This is because there is a greater danger of overheating due to the relatively small terraria warming up more molt it is absolutely essential to make sure that the old skin does not roll up like a tourniquet on the legs and cut off the blood supply. If this happens the youngster should

A juvenile Robertson's Dwarf Chameleon, *Bradypodion gutturale*, from the Cape region of South Africa. Like the young of most livebearing chameleons, it must fend for itself within minutes of birth.

rapidly and because youngsters do not tolerate as high a temperature as the adults.

In the small enclosures it is very difficult to ensure that one corner is always dry. The simplest solution is to spray only the leaves and not the branches or animals. This is important when the little chameleons shed, for when they must always run through the moisture the freshly shed old skin will not come loose and fungus infections or the buildup of water between the old and new skin can occur. Either one will soon lead to death. Furthermore, during the

be given assistance to complete the shed. It also is important at the completion of the molt to make sure that the feet are free of remnants of skin; if not, the pieces should be removed carefully with the fingernail. This is a difficult job that sometimes has to be carried out over several hours if the chameleon becomes too agitated. The growth of most offspring is not regular, but rather proceeds in steps.

Books on the terrarium hobby often end the chapter on chameleons with the advice not to keep the animals. We believe that a

Above: No, this is not a hatchling. This is a fully grown adult *Brookesia peyrierasi* on the tip of a kitchen match. Photo: R. Zobel.

recommendation of this kind is not necessary—if the potential keeper can be sure that all the technical requirements of chameleon care (including caging, maintenance, feeding, proper environmental control, proper breeding care) can be met. Whoever decides to keep the chameleons and can keep them under proper conditions will get a lot of pleasure from chameleons.

Above: *Chamaeleo campani* is very similar to the Carpet Chameleon, but notice the three white stripes on the side, each very sharply marked. Photo: R. D. Bartlett.

Below: A female Panther Chameleon, *Chamaeleo pardalis*, laying her clutch of eggs. Photo: W. Schmidt.

The best advice we can give to the beginner is to acquire captive-bred stock through a reputable dealer— beware of wild-caught animals being sold as captive-bred. You should set up the terrarium and the required food cultures beforehand as well as read the literature carefully, for only in this way will you be spared many negative experiences. A captive-bred chameleon may be expensive and its proper care and feeding will not be especially cheap, factors to be considered when thinking of buying a new pet.

Above: The female *Chamaeleo nasutus* is under 3 inches (7.5 cm) long. This probably is the smallest species of *Chamaeleo* known. Of course it is from Madagascar. Photo: R. D. Bartlett.
Below: A gorgeous adult male Veiled Chameleon, *Chamaeleo calyptratus*, with a fully developed casque. In the last few years this has become one of the most popular chameleons. Restricted to oases in Yemen, this species grows to at least 15 inches (37.5 cm). Photo: P. Freed.

BEHAVIOR

THE INDIVIDUALISTS: BEHAVIORAL OBSERVATIONS

All chameleons are active during the day. Depending on the prevailing temperatures in their biotope, the period of peak activity usually is in the morning or late afternoon hours, or both. At these times the animals run actively through the terrarium and search for food; they usually spend the rest of the time perched on a branch waiting for prey (they are said to be ambush predators).

The opinion that chameleons are slow, sluggish animals is true of only a few species. The Carpet Chameleon, in particular, which among other places inhabits the meadows in the central highlands of Madagascar, moves about as fast as common lizards in knee-high grass, so that it takes a lot of effort to catch the animals. When chameleons are disturbed in the wild, they display a lot of behavior

patterns that they lose quite quickly in captivity. Though the Brookesiinae primarily play dead when confronted by a predator, the Chamaeleoninae are almost always active. They exhibit behavior patterns like flight, disappearing behind a branch, and attack. The individual species are highly variable in their degree of aggressiveness; this subject will

be discussed in the species descriptions. In general, however, it can be said that in all species the aggressiveness is most strongly expressed toward conspecifics, followed by aggressive behavior toward other chameleon species. The aggressiveness toward other animals is slight in comparison. The individual distances are also correspondingly variable. Thus, as a general rule, the true

Below: Two Jackson's Chameleons, *Chamaeleo jacksonii*, engaged in a ritual fight. As a rule, the fights end without bloodshed. Photo: U. Friederich.

chameleons cannot be kept together. On the other hand, it is possible to keep a true chameleon with a ground (*Brookesia* or *Rhampholeon*) chameleon. If another animal comes within the individual distance of the chameleon, it will be threatened and attacked immediately by the lively species. The threatening is done through rearing up, opening the mouth wide, swaying from side to side, hissing, and turning a flattened side in the direction of the rival. While doing this the chameleon holds on with the hind feet so that it can move its whole body forward. If the intruder does not flee, the chameleon rushes forward, seizes it, and tries through an abrupt movement of the head to toss it aside, to bite it, or to push it away with the top of the head (especially in species with large head ornaments).

When a male chameleon discovers another chameleon, he starts to nod. It is uncertain if this constitutes threat or courtship behavior. If the other chameleon is also a male, he tries to intimidate

the rival by opening the mouth wide, hissing, rearing up, or making his coloration paler. If the other male reciprocates the threat behavior, a ritual fight can take place. In some species, such as *Chamaeleo pardalis*, the intimidation only lasts a short

they are forcibly kept together in captivity often leads to the death of the defeated animal, either through the direct attacks of the dominant male or because the defeated male falls into a kind of submissive behavior pattern, hardly eats anymore, and soon

PHOTO COURTESY OF DURA PRO PRODUCTS

Some type of climbing branch must be present in any *Chamaeleo* terrarium. This "Lizard Loft" rope branch would serve as well as a real branch for any lizard of appropriate size.

time and the animals almost immediately attack each other. The defeated male takes on a dark coloration and, pursued by the other male, runs for cover. Usually, however, no fighting even takes place, because the smaller animal flees immediately. The aggressiveness of males among themselves when

dies of stress. Chameleons are individuals and—apart from mating time—must be kept singly.

When a male encounters a female, he recognizes her by the absence of intimidation behavior. The male ceases his threat display and instead immediately starts to court the female. If the female is not in breeding condition and is some distance from the male, she avoids the encounter by bobbing or shaking her head and running away. If the distance is small,

Left: A gorgeous *Bradypodion thamnobates*, the Natal Midlands Dwarf Chameleon, using its specialized feet and prehensile tail to "hide in plain sight" on a slender branch. Photo: J. Visser.

she threatens by opening her mouth wide, flattening her body, hissing, swaying back and forth, and rushing forward in the male's direction, usually in combination with a warning coloration. If the male approaches anyway, he is bitten by the female. It appears that in some chameleon species a kind of restraint against biting females is present in males. Instead, they try to ward off the female just with vigorous bobbing movements. If the female is in breeding condition, however, she usually does not react to the male, but instead moves away slowly. The male lightens his ground color and runs after the female while bobbing his head and moving his body jerkily. When the male has overtaken the female, the female accepts her fate quietly, so that

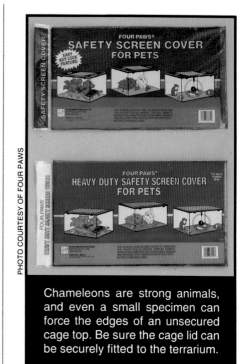

PHOTO COURTESY OF FOUR PAWS

Chameleons are strong animals, and even a small specimen can force the edges of an unsecured cage top. Be sure the cage lid can be securely fitted to the terrarium.

the male can mount. At the male's touch the female clasps the substrate firmly and lifts her tail slightly so that the male can insert the base of his tail under the female's. Only then does the female open her cloaca so that mating can take place. The length of copulation is quite variable in different chameleon species. After mating, the lizards usually perch motionless side by side for a while before they

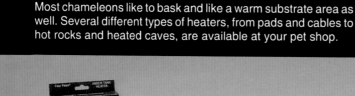

Most chameleons like to bask and like a warm substrate area as well. Several different types of heaters, from pads and cables to hot rocks and heated caves, are available at your pet shop.

PHOTO COURTESY OF FOUR PAWS

go their separate ways.

The situation is somewhat different with the ground chameleons. Thanks to their good camouflage and their retiring habits, we have only been able to make fragmentary observations of them in our terraria. Male ground chameleons usually start to court when they spot a female. If the female is not ready to breed, she indicates this by bobbing or shaking her head, whereupon the males immediately stop courting. When the female is ready to breed, however, she does not react to the male at all. The animals spend the whole day perched side by side, always

A terrarium lining provides secure footing for your chameleon.

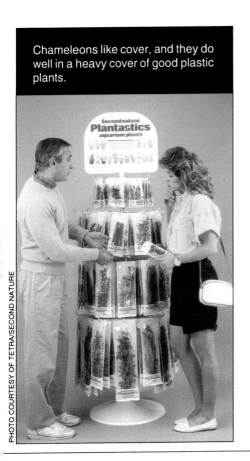

Chameleons like cover, and they do well in a heavy cover of good plastic plants.

accompanied by interludes of courtship by the male. Courtship resembles the courtship of other chameleons and includes head bobbing and jerky movements. Only toward evening, usually before the lights are turned out, does the male mount the female and mating take place. *Brookesia minima* exhibits a very unusual behavior. When the female is ready to mate, the male mounts her and, in the same way as frogs and toads, allows himself to be carried through the terrarium by the female for the whole day, sometimes for several days. Mating also takes place in the evening hours. This brief description shows clearly that the Brookesiinae are interesting objects of study. Detailed and more comprehensive descriptions of the behavior of

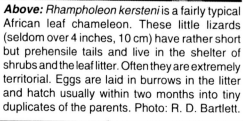

Above: *Rhampholeon kersteni* is a fairly typical African leaf chameleon. These little lizards (seldom over 4 inches, 10 cm) have rather short but prehensile tails and live in the shelter of shrubs and the leaf litter. Often they are extremely territorial. Eggs are laid in burrows in the litter and hatch usually within two months into tiny duplicates of the parents. Photo: R. D. Bartlett.

Even more leaf-like is *Rhampholeon brachyura* from the Kenya and Tanzania area. These little chameleons often allow themselves to slowly float to the ground like a dead leaf to fool predators. Photo: J. Visser.

R. D. BARTLETT

Even young chameleons are very territorial. This subadult Panther Chameleon, *Chamaeleo pardalis*, would not share a terrarium with any other chameleon.

A large male Parson's Chameleon, *Chamaeleo parsoni*, can be a vicious adversary if put in a terrarium with a smaller male. Always be very careful about caging two chameleons together.

R. D. BARTLETT

K. H. SWITAK

Namaqua Chameleons, *Chamaeleo namaquensis*, inhabit some of the driest deserts in southwestern Africa. Largely terrestrial, they lay their eggs in burrows often 10 inches (25 cm) deep near scrubby vegetation.

chameleons can be found in, among others, Schuster (1979) and Kaestle (1967).

Ground chameleons exhibit another interesting behavior pattern: a high-frequency vibrating of the body that is noticeable as soon as the animals are held in the hand. The purpose of this behavior has yet to be explained, but it possibly serves to drive off potential predators such as ants. It could, however, also be a form of communication; it is possible that the sexes find each other on the basis of this peculiar trembling. This behavior is also performed in the state of akinesis (Schmidt, Henkel, and Boehme, 1989).

The young of several species display an unusual behavior that Kaestle (1967) described for newborn *Bradypodion pumilum*, *Chamaeleo hoehnelii*, and *Chamaeleo elliotti*. The youngsters of these species, in contrast to the adults, run around for hours with short breaks so as to scatter over the largest possible area. This behavior is not observed in freshly hatched young of the *Furcifer* group. It appears that the young of these species move just far enough away from one another that they can no longer see their siblings. They must do this, however, because they are absolutely unsociable. This is displayed even during hatching.

W. SCHMIDT

A female Carpet Chameleon, *Chamaeleo lateralis*, threatens a male approaching too close.

In an incubator standing in the light, the next baby Carpet Chameleon did not hatch until the one that had already hatched had been removed. These two sat in opposite corners of the incubator, as far apart as possible.

In summary, it can be said that all chameleons are very aggressive (particularly within the species) and easily stressed animals. They are by nature solitary, and very few would survive forced association outside the breeding season. This specific idiosyncrasy of chameleons absolutely must be taken into consideration when keeping them in the terrarium!

Rhampholeon kersteni has a rather long tail for an African leaf chameleon. These chameleons closely resemble the Madagascan species of *Brookesia*.

R. D. BARTLETT

R. D. BARTLETT

This dwarf chameleon, *Bradypodion*, probably is a juvenile or a female lacking the higher crests of males. Notice the odd scales forming the crest under the throat, typical of many *Bradypodion* species.

KEEPING AND CARE

Because large numbers of wild-caught chameleons are imported each year, especially from Madagascar and West Africa, you might be led to believe that chameleons are abundant animals in our terraria. This is certainly not the case. Anyone who is familiar with the difficulties associated with keeping chameleons can imagine how many of the imported animals lived for very long after they arrived at the importer's facilities and how many survived for long in the hands of the average hobbyist. These are highly territorial animals that cannot be crowded or they will be killed by stress. Almost all chameleons live with parasites, which multiply dramatically in animals that have been weakened in shipping and can be an additional cause of death. The hobbyist who buys a chameleon in such pitiful condition will scarcely have a chance of keeping it alive for more than one or two months. This is how the story of the difficulty of keeping chameleons arose. In the following paragraphs we will discuss the important criteria for keeping them alive and healthy in captivity.

THE TERRARIUM

The ideal location of a terrarium for the majority of chameleon species should be exposed to direct sunlight only in the morning or late afternoon hours. Otherwise chameleons are highly susceptible to overheating. In the case of ground chameleons, in fact, the terrarium must be set up such that it can never be reached by the sun. Rooms with a southern exposure are only conditionally suitable for keeping highland forms, because in summer the temperatures there can get too high. In the summer it is best to keep the terrarium outside.

Unfortunately, no universal terrarium is available to us for keeping and breeding. Rather, each terrarium must be built, furnished, and maintained according to the requirements of the species being kept.

The most useful and easiest to obtain terraria are the all-glass aquaria glued together with

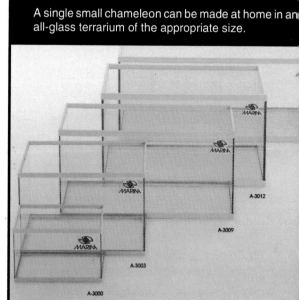

A single small chameleon can be made at home in an all-glass terrarium of the appropriate size.

PHOTO COURTESY OF HAGEN

silicone cement. Any pet shop will have a good stock of a variety of sizes and shapes for sale at reasonable prices and can order specially made terraria for you as well.

All chameleons prefer very wide terraria over narrow ones. The ability to retreat to the rear of the terrarium contributes substantially to the well-being of the lizard. The required size of the terrarium is dependent on the size and temperament of the animal (for particulars see the species descriptions in Volume 1). For tree- and bush-dwelling chameleons, terraria that are higher than long or deep are suitable. For ground-dwellers, terraria that are longer and deeper than high are appropriate. Most of the terraria that are available on the market

Full color plastic backgrounds can be used behind the chameleon terrarium.

are suitable only for terrestrial chameleons, but it is not hard or expensive to have taller terraria specially made for you.

Ventilation openings are important in the selection of the terrarium. Especially in small terraria, ventilation openings allow the humidity, temperature, and fresh-air requirements of the chameleons to be regulated. The often expressed opinion that chameleons need a great deal of "fresh air" is true of only a few species. Poor ventilation often was used to explain away illnesses and errors in maintenance such as stress and excessive temperatures. For all chameleons it is essential that a ventilation grating be present in the cover, the side, or the front so that the air cannot stagnate. If the size of the ventilation opening is increased, the relative humidity falls. If the size of the opening is decreased, the humidity rises. Rainforest dwellers, including most ground and leaf chameleons, need for their well-being a relative humidity of 100 percent at night and 70 to 100 percent during the day. This can be achieved only in terraria built with small ventilation openings and sprayed frequently and thoroughly. For certain African chameleons from the uplands, terraria built with a wood or aluminum framework and with gauze on all sides are well-suited. Opaque partitions of some type (towels work well) must be placed between adjacent terraria to prevent visual contact between neighbors.

The terraria we use for most of

A small plastic terrarium or aquarium can serve as a holding container for a baby chameleon. Remember that babies are just as aggressive as adults.

our chameleons are made of glass. The sides and the rear wall are covered with glued sheets of cork or a full color plastic background and the bottom also can be covered with cork. Otherwise all of the usual materials can serve as a substrate. With some species it has proved beneficial to glue a small, flat, rough stone to a side or the back wall; the chameleon uses this to rub off its loose skin when shedding. The furnishings consist of a lot of climbing branches that help divide the interior space and satisfy the lizard's urge to climb. One spot is somewhat more thickly planted and serves as a refuge for the chameleon, otherwise a few climbing plants round out the decorations. If terraria are set up on opposite walls of a room, care must be taken that no visual contact results. If need be, a curtain can be drawn between the terraria.

SPECIAL NEEDS

Now to the special requirements that must be met for particular groups of chameleons. Females of the egg-laying species must be mentioned first. So that they can bury their eggs without disturbance, depending on size they need a substrate of varying depth. A bottom layer of perlite or tiny plastic pellets covered with 10 to 30 centimeters (4 to 12 inches) of a slightly moist mixture of sand and peat has proved effective. (Do not use plastic pellets with small ground chameleons.) Without suitable conditions for laying the eggs, the female will retain them and eventually will die as a result of the decomposing eggs. In a few species the females do not bury the eggs at all or a flowerpot is sufficient. These species, however, are in the minority.

With the ground chameleons it is best to dispense with a substrate and instead glue sheets of cork to the bottom. On top of this is placed a layer of cork shavings, through which the lizards like to run and in which the females lay their eggs. This layer acts as a substitute for the leaf litter of their natural habitat. Naturally, female ground chameleons also bury their eggs in real leaf litter when such a substrate is available, but it then is very hard to find the eggs, which is why leaf litter should not be used.

Any number of different small containers and terraria are suitable for rearing small chameleons. Modified food-storage containers are most often used because they are easy to keep on hand in a wide variety of sizes and shapes. Transparent rectangular plastic containers with dimensions of at least 12 cm long x 12 cm deep x 18 cm high (5 x 5 x 7 inches) are good. The top is cut out completely and fine wire mesh is glued over the opening. An additional hole can be cut in one side and covered with gauze. A sheet of cork or printed plastic background is glued to the opposite side so that the containers can be placed side by side without having visual contact with the neighboring container. The decorations consist of small branches and a climbing plant such as *Ficus pumila*. After a fluorescent tube has been placed on top of the container, the rearing container is ready for use. If the temperatures in the containers are too low, they can be heated easily from below with a heating cable— but take care, because the little

A Flap-necked Chameleon, *Chamaeleo dilepis*, showing excitement coloration.

L. BINDEWALD

chameleons die quickly of overheating! So that the whole thing does not look simply like a messy collection of containers, the containers can be placed neatly in an attractive cabinet.

For the hobbyist who has little chameleons regularly and in numbers, it is worthwhile to build a permanent rearing installation. Our rearing installations consist of long terraria divided into small rearing enclosures. The smallest recommended size is a small terrarium with dimensions of 10 cm long x 10 cm deep x 30 cm high (4 x 4 x 12 inches), which can be expanded easily as the small chameleons grow, up to a size of 20 cm long x 20 cm deep x 50 cm high (8 x 8 x 20 inches).

Terraria 10 cm long x 15 cm deep x 50 cm high (4 x 6 x 20 inches) have proved to be particularly effective. Because of the great danger of overheating, the whole cover and a broad strip in front should be used for ventilation. For lighting we use fluorescent tubes exclusively in the time following hatching, and not until later is a small spotlight installed to supplement the available light. Friederich offers her offspring the mild warmth of a 25-watt lamp from the start. The setup and furnishings are exactly the same as those of the large terraria.

All newly acquired animals

should be handled with great care at first. With chameleons a fairly long quarantine period in a special terrarium is unavoidable. All of the usual terraria can be used as quarantine cages, particularly the plastic tanks available on the market. The furnishings should be as simple as possible: a substrate of newspaper, a potted plant, and a few branches. If a parasitic infestation is present, everything should be thrown out after the quarantine period and treatments are finished. A plant must be

The true *Chamaeleo bitaeniatus*, the Two-striped Chameleon, is very similar to *Chamaeleo ellioti* but has a more irregular dorsal crest. This is one of the most colorful chameleons and a livebearer to boot.

K. PAYSAN

present, otherwise the weakened animals would be subject to constant stress in the absence of hiding places and this would weaken them even more. During the acclimation phase the hobbyist should check to see that the animals are feeding and drinking satisfactorily and whether injuries are present. It is advisable to have the droppings tested for parasites several times during the quarantine period.

A few chameleon species are suitable for keeping at liberty in rooms and greenhouses that meet their requirements. Some chameleons do well in well-planted windowsill greenhouses. A few points, however, must be observed. For example, a spotlight must be installed under which the lizard can bask at any time. A food dish should be put in a place where the chameleon can easily get at it and see into it. Because the relative humidity is lower in the room than in the terrarium, a free-ranging chamaeleon must be given water to drink regularly. The water requirement will be covered adequately if the plants are sprayed a little every day and the lizard is given water every other day. It is essential that the room where chameleons are kept at liberty be entered cautiously, first looking at the floor—many chameleons are not afraid to run around on the floor and it is all too easy to step on an animal or to crush it with an inward-opening door. In this case a mirror installed on the floor next to the door can be used to look behind the door when it is only slightly open.

Pregnant females of the egg-laying species present a problem. Several days before they lay their eggs they start searching for a suitable laying place. We doubtless do not have to describe what a planted windowsill greenhouse looks like after numerous test holes have been dug by a female *Chamaeleo pardalis*. It is advisable to place a fertile female in a suitable terrarium immediately after mating and to leave her there until the eggs have been laid.

HEATING

Species that come from extremely hot regions are particularly well suited for keeping in greenhouses, which heat up in the sun and cool at night. Special microclimates (cool, moist corners) must be provided for the chameleons kept there so

U. FRIEDERICH

A dwarf chameleon, probably *Bradypodion gutturale*, in excellent color. These little chameleons may be the best choice for beginners because they are hardy and are livebearers.

they can retreat to cover when it gets too hot. The greenhouse must be heated so the temperature at night does not fall below 10°C (50°F). A disadvantage of this method of keeping is that it is very difficult to find egg clutches, because the female chameleons usually camouflage the laying site very well; it would be best to remove egg-bearing females to separate terraria. An advantage of this type of keeping is that it is possible to keep several animals together without the chameleons seeing one another at all times. This is a big advantage during the breeding season, for then the animals can mate when they want, which has a positive effect on the number of fertile

An unusual blue form of the Panther Chameleon, *Chamaeleo pardalis*, from Nosy Be.

K. LIEBE

Most chameleons enjoy basking. Your pet shop will have several excellent types of basking lights for sale.

eggs.

We have mentioned so often the danger of overheating that we now have to say something about the opposite. Low temperatures are in general tolerated better than excessively high ones, but caution is advised here. For example, *Chamaeleo pardalis* does not tolerate temperatures below 12°C (54°F). It is not necessarily advisable to mimic the prevailing nocturnal temperature. Rather, a healthy medium seems to be the right strategy for successful keeping. During the day the temperatures should always be in the range of the activity temperature. In addition, however, a source of heat such as a spotlight or other type of basking light must always be present under which the chameleon can warm itself to the preferred temperature. For the well-being of the lizard it is absolutely necessary to lower the temperature at night. In the terrarium this is achieved simply by turning off the lighting and the heating. Because the daytime temperatures are on average about 25°C (77°F) and nighttime temperatures in the home are on average about 16 to 18°C (60 to 65°F), the nighttime decrease is about 7 to 9°C (10 to 15°F), which usually is adequate. The nocturnal drop in temperature seems to be essential for restful sleep; this is probably due to the decrease in the metabolic rate. If a chameleon species that is used to very strong cooling during the night in the wild is not offered cool nights, the lizard will exhibit a sharp decrease in vitality and will have a shorter life expectancy.

There are a number of different ways to heat the terrarium. Small terraria are most easily heated with a heating cable and large terraria with Reptile Brightlights, spotlights, or halogen lights. With the normal spotlight reflectors it is best to choose those of between 15 and 40 watts and with the halogen lights those of 20 watts. The lights should be installed such that when the chameleons "sun" themselves they cannot touch the bulbs; otherwise the scales could be burned slightly. For this reason it is important to make sure when decorating the terrarium that a distance of at least 4 centimeters (1.6 inches) is always maintained between the animal and the lamp. This is achieved by making sure that the branches are not positioned too close to the lamp. Terraria lighted with mercury-vapor or similar lamps usually do not require supplemental heating, because the lamps give off a great deal of heat. The fear is often voiced that the chameleons could shoot their tongue against the lamp and injure it in this way. We have used spotlights and lamps in our terraria for years without ever having seen a chameleon shoot its tongue against a lamp.

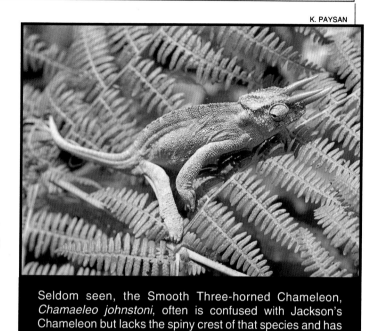

K. PAYSAN

Seldom seen, the Smooth Three-horned Chameleon, *Chamaeleo johnstoni*, often is confused with Jackson's Chameleon but lacks the spiny crest of that species and has more regular scalation. It lays eggs, while Jackson's gives live-birth.

ARTIFICIAL SUN?

When you consider that in the tropics sunlight has an intensity of 100,000 lux, and even in the shade of a tree it is still 10,000 lux, it is clear how hard it is even to approximate the natural conditions of your charges. Most chameleons worship the sun." The light intensity therefore plays an important role for their hunting behavior and also contributes to the increased vitality of the animals. Schuster (1979) showed for Jackson's Chameleon *Chamaeleo jacksonii*) that a light intensity of at least 100 lux is required for the successful capture of food animals. A 40-watt incandescent bulb produces only 35 lux at a distance of one meter (1.1 yards). It can be readily observed that chameleons do not display their entire behavioral repertoire unless a certain minimal light intensity is present. Hobbyists who can keep their chameleons in greenhouses have it the easiest, for even in a windowsill greenhouse there usually is a light intensity of only 2000 lux.

To illuminate the terrarium, powerful fluorescent tubes (of the type made specifically for use with reptiles) as well as mercury-vapor and halogen lamps are suitable. For small rearing containers a single fluorescent tube is sufficient, for terraria with a height of 50 centimeters (20 inches) at least two fluorescent tubes are

P. FREED

Chamaeleo willisi is another of the unusual Madagascan chameleons imported on a sporadic basis. This species inhabits the canopy, so it is not easily collected until the trees are cut, which unfortunately is happening in most forested regions of Madagascar.

necessary, and for higher terraria correspondingly more light is needed. Stettler (1973) says that four to six fluorescent tubes are needed for a terrarium with the dimensions 70 cm long x 40 cm deep x 75 cm high (28 x 16 x 30 inches). If the terraria are even higher, only metal-vapor lamps can still do the job. High-intensity mercury-vapor lamps have proved to be particularly effective. When they are installed inside the terrarium cover, no light is lost and simultaneously a good source of heat for the terrarium is available. The new iodine-vapor lamps produce considerably more light than do mercury-vapor lamps. This kind of lamp almost seems to have been created precisely for sun worshipers. They are available in sizes starting at 35 watts, but unfortunately they are very expensive. This is to some extent compensated for by their long life and low electricity use.

Only "daylight" lamps should be used, because they produce a color spectrum most similar to that of the sun and have the most agreeable light for our eyes. With fluorescent tubes a combination of "daylight" and "warm tone" tubes has proved to be the most attractive. It is also important to use good-quality reflectors (available in pet shops). With their use the light output can easily be increased by 40 percent. The halogen spotlights that have been available for some time are ideal as point sources of light to supplement the output of the fluorescent tubes. Unfortunately, they require the use of a transformer, so it is worthwhile to buy them only when they are to be used with several terraria.

The light period should either mimic the natural conditions or be maintained at a constant 12 to 14 hours a day (except for *Chamaeleo chamaeleon*; see volume 1). We have had good experiences with keeping chameleons in the garden in the summer. It is readily apparent how the animals are revived in the sun—their colors become brighter and their activity increases. Suitable terraria for outdoor keeping can be constructed with wire mesh and located in a wind-protected place in partial sun (guard against overheating during the day and cats and rats at night). Chameleons should not be allowed to run free in the garden, because in only a few minutes they will have disappeared for good!

The use of ultraviolet lamps is often recommended. Some even consider it to be essential and others at least attribute a vitalizing effect to it. We have bred chameleons over several generations without the use of ultraviolet lamps of any kind without noticing any adverse effects on our charges. With adequate doses of vitamin D3, in our opinion you can safely dispense with the use of ultraviolet lamps. The very horny skin of chameleons lets less than one percent of the ultraviolet rays through anyway.

In closing, it bears repeating that many chameleon species make differing demands with respect to lighting. This will be discussed in more detail in the descriptions of the species in volume 1.

TECHNICAL AIDS

Today, timers are a must for any kind of terrarium keeping, for no

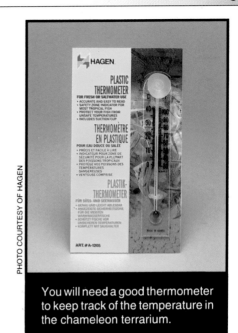

PHOTO COURTESY OF HAGEN

You will need a good thermometer to keep track of the temperature in the chameleon terrarium.

one has the time to turn the light or heat on or off at the same time each day. With their aid a kind of regularity can be achieved that is beneficial for the well-being of the chameleons. Through trial and error it is possible, for example, to determine exactly when and for how long the heating must remain switched on so that the temperature does not fall too much or stay too high. Thermostats also are available that can be used to switch the lights and ventilation fans on and off when pre-set temperatures are reached. If all this were done by hand, maintaining a terrarium would certainly be a time-consuming task.

Recently, automatic sprinklers have come into more widespread use in terraria, and with them it is possible to reduce the daily workload to a true minimum. The only daily manual activity left to be

P. FREED

A good look at a rare chameleon, *Chamaeleo deremensis* from Tanzania. There are several horned chameleons, though only a few species make it to the hobby. The number of horns may vary from one to four, sometimes varying within a species. Look for other characters (such as scalation and crests) when identifying chameleons.

performed is the feeding and supplemental watering of the animals. This leaves a lot of time to observe and study the chameleons. At the same time, an automatic sprinkler also leaves more free time for the owner, who does not have to be present every day and can go away for an occasional weekend without having to worry about the chameleons.

DIET

Feeding chameleons is no longer a problem today. A good assortment of different food insects can be purchased in any pet shop catering to reptiles. Insects collected in the wild should not be fed because of the danger of possible contamination with insecticides as well as for reasons of conservation.

The cheapest way to obtain food is to rear it yourself, though this can be a time-consuming occupation and often requires a great deal of space, as well as an initial investment in containers and food for the insect. By raising your own insects, though, you will know how good and nutritious the food insects are. Because the assortment of different insects that can be reared in captivity is meager in comparison with the supply found in the wild, special attention must be paid to providing a varied and all-around diet. Only in this way will the chameleons be assured a balanced diet.

There are numerous books on the subject of rearing food animals, but none on "rational food rearing," for most of the descriptions in the literature are much too complicated and time consuming for the average reptile keeper.

A cheap type of food animal that can serve as a supplement to the main food animals (crickets, grasshoppers, and cockroaches) is large flies. The easiest way to obtain flies is to buy a pack of maggots (gentles) at a bait shop and keep them in a warm place so that the maggots pupate and the flies emerge about 14 days later. The flies are then kept in large plastic containers (with a volume of at least 3 liters, almost a gallon) for at least three days and fed a mixture of molasses, powdered milk, baby cereal, and vitaminized drinking water. Finally they are fortified with a vitamin and mineral supplement and fed to the lizards. Some chameleon species go downright crazy for flies.

A good food animal is the green cockroach (other species can be used but there is a chance of escapes and contamination so it is best to use a delicate, more tropical species in case accidents happen) because under certain

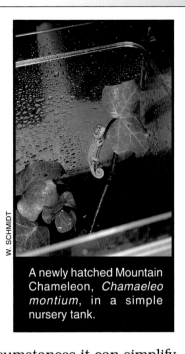

W. SCHMIDT

A newly hatched Mountain Chameleon, *Chamaeleo montium*, in a simple nursery tank.

circumstances it can simplify chameleon keeping. The colony of green cockroaches (possibly a *Panchlora* species) is kept in a tightly closed terrarium with a bottom layer of garden soil or small animal litter about 10 centimeters (4 inches) deep. This substrate must always be kept wet. Caution is advised when working in the rearing container, because the adults can fly. On this layer are placed one or two egg cartons and a few banana skins, which must be replaced once a week. In addition, a little honey must always be fed. The more cockroaches, the more banana skins or pieces of banana must be fed. Old food should always be removed because of the danger that too many mites will propagate in the rearing container. The temperature should be kept at a constant 38°C (100°F). The reproductive cycle is very long, but your patience will be rewarded because a highly coveted and attractive food animal is obtained. They are best fed only with the feeding forceps or from a dissecting needle. Rearing is not as productive as with other cockroach cultures.

In general, chameleons eat all live insects. We feed various crickets, cockroaches, grasshoppers, flies, wax and flour moths, flour beetles, mealworms, black beetle larvae, slugs, isopods, and spiders. As a first food for baby chameleons we offer fruitflies (*Drosophila*), the smallest crickets, and springtails. A few large chameleon species will take baby mice. A few readily eaten food animals cannot be recommended for obvious reasons. Females of *Chamaeleo pardalis*, for example, like to eat small gecko species. A captive female Panther Chameleon was observed feeding on young *Epipedobates tricolor*. *Chamaeleo fischeri* eats small *Anolis* species. The true lizard-eaters, like *Chamaeleo brevicornis* and *Chamaeleo melleri*, will not miss a gecko. The Veiled Chameleon, *Chamaeleo calyptratus*, is known to eat *Bradypodion pumilum* in captivity. In several regions in Madagascar the natives bring large *Chamaeleo oustaleti* into their gardens and houses so that they will eat all of the "vermin."

FEEDING PROBLEMS

Unfortunately, some chameleon species become very fussy with respect to food in captivity. After a short period of transition, they may refuse to eat anything but their favorite foods. You must never allow things to get to this point.

The problem can be avoided by offering the most varied diet possible. Almost all chameleons have a special liking for green food insects. Even the fussiest eater, as often is the case with recently imported animals, gives in when it catches sight of a green cockroach or a green grasshopper. Chameleons are fed daily with one fast day a week. How much food is required by the individual species can be found in the species descriptions.

It often is claimed that chameleons become obese in captivity. When such assertions are investigated, however, it usually turns out that the animals, perhaps because of too little water, developed a fatty kidney or the like and later died. We are aware of only a few cases of true obesity in chameleons caused by too much food with the simultaneous lavish administration of vitamins. In one instance the animal had gotten so heavy that the bones had grown crookedly. Generally, the sluggish species tend more to obesity than do the lively species. With reference to obesity, special care must be taken with females. One of our own females, which we put on a diet, died a few days later after laying eggs (the pregnancy had been overlooked). As a rule, chameleons eat only as much as they need.

Based on our observations, the most favorable feeding time for the ground chameleons is in the morning and for the true chameleons the afternoon, when the animals have warmed up completely. Large chameleons should be acclimated to the feeding forceps or to a food bowl from which they can "shoot" at the insects. Not all individuals get used to this, and with very shy animals the live insects must be dumped into the terrarium to be hunted down at the lizard's leisure. With the small species and youngsters, we shake an appropriate number of *Drosophila* or small crickets into the terrarium once a day.

Unfortunately, chameleons occasionally must be force-fed. With many species this is very easy. As soon as the chameleon is taken from the terrarium it opens its mouth, and the food or medicine can be pushed deep enough into the gullet. If the animal does not open its mouth willingly, it can be irritated by stroking it, tapping on its mouth, or pressing lightly on its eyes to force it to open the mouth. If the chameleon continues to refuse, it can be exposed to the sight of one of its conspecifics. If even this is unsuccessful, it is better to leave the animal alone.

L. BINDEWALD

Large chameleons, like this Jackson's, *Chamaeleo jacksonii*, can dispatch relatively large insect prey with tough chitinous skeletons. Other chameleons will take only the smallest and most delicate insects.

It often is claimed that chameleons are strictly insect-eaters or at least carnivores. This is not true. We have observed individual animals of the following species actively feeding on plants: *Chamaeleo calyptratus*, *Chamaeleo brevicornis*, *Chamaeleo lateralis*, and *Chamaeleo pardalis*. Shortly after it was placed in a terrarium, the *Chamaeleo calyptratus* bit off and ate several pieces of a philodendron. We suspected at the time that it had been so thirsty after the long transport that it wanted to meet its water requirement through plant parts. It continued, however, to regularly eat small pieces from a leaf. Later this behavior was also shown by its offspring. Henkel filmed a *Chamaeleo brevicornis* in the wild literally grazing on the yellow flowers on a bush. In the terrarium, Seume was the first to observe a *Chamaeleo lateralis* feeding regularly on the leaves of *Zebrina pendula*. Our initial suspicion that this was merely a question of an isolated feat of an individual chameleon was not confirmed. The same plant also is eaten regularly by other Carpet and Panther Chameleons, but strangely not by all individuals. Therefore, we can recommend *Zebrina pendula* as a terrarium plant. Furthermore, *Chamaeleo brevicornis* has also been observed feeding on fern leaves in the terrarium. Examinations of the stomach contents of wild chameleons have also revealed the presence of vegetable remains and seeds. This shows that more observations are needed.

SUPPLEMENTS

Now on to an important topic that has been discussed frequently in the specialist literature—supplying calcium and vitamins. We will dispense with listing the many recipes and instead would like to describe briefly our recipe for all those who do not have one yet. Anyone who has already kept and bred chameleons successfully for years should stick to his or her recipe, for a universal recipe certainly does not exist.

All—and we really do mean all, without exception—food animals are well dusted with a mixture of

PHOTO COURTESY OF FOUR PAWS

Since chameleons often take their water by licking dew and droplets on the leaves, spray vitamins may be a good choice for presenting supplements.

calcium and vitamins. In addition, every week the animals receive, depending on size, up to 5 drops of liquid multivitamin directly in the mouth. To the drinking water (with smaller species and youngsters, the spraying water) is added more liquid multivitamins, one teaspoon of calcium gluconate per 5 liters of water, and less than one drop of iodine solution twice a week. We decided to give iodine supplements after enlarged thyroid glands turned up in individual youngsters. In addition, the chameleons should be offered a small dish with cuttlebone or a reptile calcium supplement. Individual chameleons have repeatedly been observed actively taking up calcium.

WATER

We basically meet the water requirement through spraying. There are only two exceptions. Large animals, starting with the size of a full-grown *Chamaeleo lateralis* (total length approximately 15 centimeters, 6 inches), receive water from a pipette twice a week. With chameleons that do not drink voluntarily, we simply spray water directly into their mouths. Furthermore, animals in quarantine tanks must be given

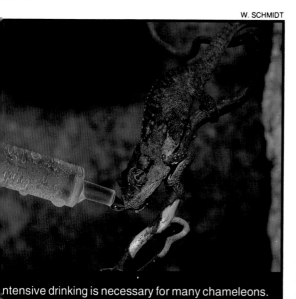

W. SCHMIDT

ntensive drinking is necessary for many chameleons. Specimens in quarantine tanks must be given water every other day, and they must be made to drink from a pipette and not a spray.

regulator. The flask is filled with water and hung over the terrarium, then the infusion regulator is attached and the drip rate adjusted. The water does not have to drip the whole day; an hour in late afternoon is sufficient. Unfortunately, there usually is not enough room above the terrarium and, additionally, the terrarium room ends up looking like an intensive care unit. Individual chameleons might take water from automatic drinkers for small animals, but unfortunately very few do. It is up to the individual hobbyist to do some testing.

A little tip about planting: There are plants, such as the bird's nest fern, that allow large drops to form under the leaves after spraying, the drops remaining hanging there longer than on most other plants. Such plants are particularly well suited as terrarium plants. Almost all chameleons like to drink from leaf axils and bromeliad cups. Unfortunately, they also like to defecate there, causing the plants to rot.

water by hand, because no spraying is done there at all, since otherwise the animals would take in their own pathogens again. Chameleons in quarantine must be given water every other day. You should get used to using a separate pipette for each chameleon and clean it after every use. Only in this way can the transmission of diseases be prevented. You also should not neglect to offer the chameleons a drinking bowl. Many get used to it and like to drink from it. On the other hand, others drink, besides drops, only moving water. For this purpose the use of an indoor fountain (commonly used in hydroculture installations) has proved to be very useful. Dripping water is also taken by many chameleons. Use an empty IV flask (available in hospitals) and the appropriate infusion

Large chameleons, like this Carpet Chameleon, *Chamaeleo lateralis*, can be given water directly from a pipette at least twice a week.

W. SCHMIDT

AID FOR ILLNESSES

This is one of the most difficult subjects in the keeping of chameleons. Because we, and most hobbyists, do not have the appropriate qualifications, we will dispense with presenting, as so often happens in the specialist literature, a table with illnesses and their treatment. When you see these tables in the terrarium literature, it is easy to come to the conclusion that diagnosis and treatment are child's play. A new, comprehensive, but quite technical, book on veterinary care of reptiles is Dr. Fredric Frye's *Reptile Care. An Atlas of Diseases and Treatments* (T.F.H. Publications, Inc.).

CHOICES

Anyone who plans to acquire a chameleon naturally will want to know the animal's state of health. There are several features to check before purchasing. The first is that the eyes must not be sunken into the eye sockets, but rather must protrude and be stretched tight. Many species can withdraw the eyes into the head and always do so when they feel threatened or are irritated. The claim that the intensity of the color is of decisive importance for judging the condition of the animal is true only under certain circumstances. Based on this advice, healthy animals should exhibit bright colors. Far more often, especially with freshly imported animals, the bright colors are a type of stress coloration. Pale colors can often be

the result of submissive behavior. Incorrect keeping conditions, such as too little light or too low temperatures, also affect the coloration. The condition of the tail actually is an accurate indication of the state of nutrition of the chameleon—it must not consist exclusively of skin and bones. Another good criterion is the activity of the animals (this applies only to lively species) under normal conditions; that is, under temperatures in the activity temperature range.

Even when all of these points are considered, a little luck is needed to purchase a truly healthy animal. Captive-bred animals are in a clearly better state of health than are imported animals, so we particularly recommend the purchase of captive-bred animals by inexperienced chameleon keepers.

After a chameleon has been acquired, it should immediately be placed in a quarantine tank and fed and watered thoroughly. Because chameleons usually carry large parasite loads, it is best to have the droppings checked by an experienced reptile veterinarian. Because it might take several days for eggs, etc., of parasites to appear in the feces, a second sample should be examined about three weeks after the first. Your local small animal veterinarian should be able to suggest a vet in your area who deals with reptiles; some vets advertise in reptile magazines. Expect to pay a fee for examination of a fecal sample.

If the second fecal sample also is negative for parasites, the chameleon should be moved to a normal terrarium. If the chameleon has parasites it should be treated according to instructions from the veterinarian, using medications that are recommended. The course of treatment (sometimes continuing for several weeks) should be followed by another analysis of the droppings.

EGG-BINDING

One of the frequent causes of losses in chameleons is egg-binding. Egg-binding occurs when a female that is filled with eggs is unable to lay them. The reasons for this include: 1) no suitable laying site; 2) too much stress, such as through frequent transferring of the female during pregnancy or being constantly in view of another chameleon; 3) an inadequate supply of vitamins and minerals; 4) organic disease, such as the blockage of an oviduct.

Numbers 1 to 3 are mistakes in keeping and should not occur if you followed instructions given earlier. Number 4 is rare, and the normal hobbyist is helpless in the face of it. If egg-binding occurs because of causes 1 to 3, the chameleon can be injected with oxytocin (see your veterinarian), with which we have had variable success. With the Carpet Chameleon (*Chamaeleo lateralis*), among other things the drastic lowering of the nighttime temperature led to the desired success. Occasionally, after a female chameleon lays eggs or gives birth a weakness in the ability to shoot out the tongue (more precisely, a paralysis of the tongue) occurs. This paralysis disappears in a few days after the administration of adequate doses of vitamin B and a good diet. Gentian violet (5% gentian violet dissolved in 70% alcohol; see your veterinarian) has proved to be the ideal disinfectant for minor wounds and injuries to the scales. The remedy is simply applied to the injury with the aid of a cotton swab.

Wild-caught chameleons are often injured on the tip of the snout. Usually a small abscess has already formed between the skin and jaw. Here the skin on the jaw must be carefully pulled down, all of the pus removed, and the site treated with an antibiotic ointment. Treatment should continue until the sore is completely healed.

Difficulties in shedding can be the result of too high or too low humidity; here experimentation is called for. It is not always serious if a chameleon does not shed completely in one day, and in some species it always takes longer. If you see, however, that the chameleon cannot shed on its own, it should be bathed for several minutes in lukewarm water and the skin can be carefully pulled off. Many keepers feel it is better not to tamper with the shed unless it becomes obvious that the chameleon cannot complete the process unassisted.

ACKNOWLEDGMENTS

We wish to give special thanks to Mrs. Ursel Friederich, Dipl. Biol., Stuttgart, for numerous suggestions and much information, and for the support that helped to ensure realization of the manuscript, as well as to Dr. W. Boehme, Bonn, for reviewing and correcting the manuscript.

We would also like to thank everyone who, through sharing information with us, contributed to the success of this book. We would like to single out the following individuals in alphabetical order: K. Assmann, Muenster; A. Graf, Beimerstetten; S. Heinecke, Wuppertal; F. W. Henkel, Bergkamen; W. Kunstek, CW Kerkrade; R. Leptien, Alveslohe; K. Liebel, Herne; V. Mueller, Soest; M. v. Niekisch, Stuttgart; J. Peitschmann, Aalen; B. Seume, Soest; H. Simon, Dreieich; K. Steffen, Kamen; R. Stockey, Hagen; R. Zobel, Herne.

Last but not least, we thank Mrs. G. Schmidt for the preparation of the original manuscript.

See Volume 1 for the complete bibliographic references to sources credited in this volume.

Expect to pay a veterinarian or pet expert for their services in examining ill chameleons.

J. R. QUINN

INDEX

Page numbers in **boldface** refer to illustrations.